CA N RAJA

Smart Funding Strategies for Entrepreneurs

A Guide to Minimise Financial Mistakes & Maximise Wealth

Contents

1

Introduction

Overview of the Importance of Smart Funding Strategies

As an entrepreneur, navigating the complex world of business financing is a critical aspect of your journey. You're already aware of the multifaceted challenges and difficulties in raising funds for running your business. Whether it's through personal savings, loans from friends and relatives, investor funding, borrowing from banks or financial institutions, or managing credit from suppliers, the sources of funds are as varied as they are vital.

These sources can be broadly classified into two categories: internal sources, such as owners' contributions, retained profits, and payables to employees; and external sources, which encompass funds raised from lenders, banks, financial institutions, suppliers, and other external entities.

At this juncture, you might wonder about the necessity of a strategic approach to funding. After all, securing the funds and channeling them into your business might seem straightforward. However, the reality is more nuanced. The funds flowing into your business are akin to a double-edged sword. They hold the potential to either propel your business to new heights or become a weight that drags it down.

This varying impact is contingent on the composition of the funds you have mobilized for your enterprise. A business operating solely on personal funds of the owner carries a different risk and reward profile compared to one that is a blend of personal and external funding. Similarly, a venture predominantly reliant on external financing faces its own unique set of challenges and opportunities.

The crux of the matter lies in how you structure the finances of your business. The intricate balance of different funding sources will play a pivotal role in determining the wealth you can generate as an owner or entrepreneur. It's not just about having access to funds; it's about strategically aligning these funds with your business objectives and growth plans.

In this book, we delve into the intricacies of smart funding strategies. We will explore how astute financial planning and tactical funding choices can lay the groundwork for a thriving business and substantial wealth creation. The journey ahead is about transforming funding from a mere necessity into a powerful tool for business success. Let's embark on this journey to understand the art and science of smart funding, the potential pitfalls to avoid, and the strategies that can make your business financially resilient and prosperous.

B. Brief Explanation of Capital Structure and Its Impact on Wealth Creation

As an entrepreneur, understanding your business's capital structure is crucial. This isn't just a term you'd come across in finance textbooks; it's a practical tool that shapes the financial backbone of your venture. Capital structure, in simple terms, is about how you mix different types of funding to finance your operations and growth. This blend usually involves a combination of debt (like loans and bonds) and equity (such as stocks or your own investment into the business).

Let's break it down:

Debt vs. Equity: When you use debt, you're borrowing money that needs to be paid back with interest. This can be cost-effective due to tax benefits, but those regular interest payments can strain your cash flow. Equity, however, means raising money by selling parts of your business. It doesn't burden your cash flow like debt does, but it does dilute your ownership.

Balancing Risk: The right capital structure is about managing risk smartly. High debt can mean higher profits when times are good, but it can also spell trouble during downturns. Too much equity might keep you free from debt, but it could also mean losing a slice of your control over the business.

Wealth Creation: Here's the key - your capital structure should be a strategic decision aimed at maximizing your business's value. You want to find the perfect balance where your costs are low and your returns are high. This can lead to an increase in the overall worth of your business, directly affecting your personal wealth as an owner.

A Dynamic Decision: Remember, there's no one-size-fits-all solution. The best capital structure for your business today might not be the best one tomorrow. It changes with your business's growth stage, market trends, and your unique needs and objectives. So, keeping an eye on this and being ready to adapt is crucial.

In essence, getting your capital structure right is not just about how you fund your business; it's about setting it up for sustainable growth and maximized wealth. This is just the beginning of our journey into the world of strategic funding. As we move forward, we'll dive deeper into how you can leverage these concepts for the success of your venture.

C. Introduction to the Fund Utilization Principle

As an entrepreneur, you know raising funds is a big part of your business. But there's something just as important that often gets missed: the Fund Utilization Principle. This is about using the money you get in the best way possible.

A Hint, Not the Whole Story: The Fund Utilization Principle helps you decide how to use short-term and long-term funds. But, I won't go into all the details right now. There's a special part of this book that will explain it fully. And it's really important.

Why You Should Care: Using your money in the wrong way

can cause big problems for your business. This isn't talked about much, but it's a big reason why many businesses fail.

Stay Curious: I'm giving you a sneak peek now, but the full story is coming later in the book. This isn't just another topic; it's a key lesson that can really help your business.

Important Lessons Ahead: The section about the Fund Utilization Principle is one of the most important parts of this book. It's not just tips and tricks; it's advice that can make a big difference for your business.

So, keep this in mind as you read on. We'll get into all the details later, and it's going to be a big help for you and your business.

2

Understanding Capital Structure

Definition and Components of Capital Structure

As an entrepreneur, you're likely already juggling a lot with your business. But there's one concept that's really worth your time – Capital Structure. This isn't just financial jargon; it's a key part of how your business will grow and succeed.

What is Capital Structure?: Let's keep it simple. Capital structure is all about how your business is funded. Think of it as the recipe for your business's financial health. It combines different ingredients – some debt here (like loans or bonds) and some equity there (like your own money or investments from others).

The Debt Component: Debt is money you borrow. It needs to be paid back with interest, but it has its perks. For instance, interest payments are tax-deductible, which can save some money. But remember, too much debt can be risky, especially if your business hits a rough patch.

The Equity Component: Equity is the money that you, as the owner, put into your business or that you get from investors. Unlike debt, you don't have to pay back equity, but it does mean sharing your profits and sometimes, a bit of control over your business.

Why It Matters: The way you mix debt and equity affects everything – from how much risk you're taking to how much control you keep over your business. It also influences how much money you can make and how your business can grow.

So, as you move forward with your venture, think of capital structure as your business's financial foundation. It's not just about getting the money to run your business; it's about choosing the right mix of debt and equity to make your business strong and profitable.

B. Importance of Finding the Right Balance between Debt and Equity

As an entrepreneur, finding the right mix of debt and equity in your business is like making a great recipe – the balance is everything. Let's talk about why getting this balance right is so important for your business.

The Debt-Equity Scale: Imagine a scale with debt on one side and equity on the other. Too much on either side, and things can get shaky. Debt means loans and money you have to pay back with interest. Equity means the money you and others invest in your business, which doesn't need to be paid back, but it can dilute your ownership.

Risks of Too Much Debt: Taking on a lot of debt can feel like a tightrope walk. Sure, it can help you grow fast, but what if things don't go as planned? High debt can mean big interest payments, and that's tough if your cash flow isn't strong. It's a bit like juggling fire – it can get risky.

Downsides of Too Much Equity: On the other hand, relying too much on equity can also have its drawbacks. It might mean giving away parts of your business to investors. More investors mean you might have to share more of your profits and even some control over how you run things.

Finding the Sweet Spot: The trick is to find that sweet spot – a balance that lets your business grow without putting too much pressure on your finances or losing too much control. It's about leveraging the advantages of both debt and equity while keeping their downsides in check.

It's Dynamic: Remember, this balance isn't a one-time thing. It changes as your business grows and as the market shifts. What works today might need tweaking tomorrow. It's an ongoing process, like tuning an instrument to keep it playing just right.

So, as you steer your business forward, keep an eye on this balance. It's not just about having enough money; it's about having the right kind of money. This balance can make a big difference in how much your business can achieve and how smoothly it runs.

In the following sections, we'll explore how to strike and maintain this balance, ensuring that your business stays financially healthy and poised for growth.

C. Case Studies on Successful Businesses with Optimal Capital Structures

In this section, we'll delve into real-world examples of companies that have either thrived or failed due to their capital structures. As an entrepreneur, understanding these cases can provide valuable insights into the importance of a balanced financial strategy.

Success Stories:

Apple Inc. (USA): Apple's optimal mix of equity and debt, with significant cash reserves and strategic use of long-term debt, showcases a balanced approach supporting growth and innovation.

Tesco PLC (UK): Tesco's stable capital structure, balancing debt and equity, allowed the company to maintain financial stability, even during economic downturns.

Reliance Industries Limited (India): With a strategic blend of internal funds and external borrowing, Reliance effectively financed large projects like Jio, revolutionizing the telecom sector in India.

Failure Cases:

Enron (USA): Enron's downfall was due to its executives using accounting loopholes to hide massive debts, leading to bankruptcy.

Kingfisher Airlines (India): High levels of debt and an unsustainable expansion strategy led to the airline's financial collapse.

As an entrepreneur, these examples offer powerful insights. Success in business isn't just about having a great product or service; it's also about how you finance your growth and manage your debts.

A well-thought-out capital structure that balances risk and growth potential is key to sustainable business success. Remember, the right capital structure for your business will depend on your specific circumstances, industry, and growth stage. It's a dynamic process that requires ongoing attention and adjustment.

3

Wealth Creation through Capital Structure

Exploring the Impact of Capital Structure on Equity Shareholder Wealth

As an entrepreneur, one of your key goals is to create wealth, not just for yourself but also for your shareholders. The capital structure of your business plays a critical role in this process.

Equity and Shareholder Value: When you use more equity in your capital structure, you're giving away a part of your company's ownership. This can be great for shareholders if your company grows, as the value of their shares increases. However, too much equity can dilute their ownership, potentially reducing the value of their investment.

Debt's Role: Debt can be a tool to leverage your business's growth without diluting equity. When used wisely, it can increase shareholder wealth as the company grows. But high debt can also increase financial risk. If things don't go as planned, shareholders could see their investment value decrease significantly.

Balancing Act: The key is finding a balance. You want enough debt to leverage growth but not so much that it puts your company at risk. A healthy balance can lead to an increase in shareholder wealth as the company grows and becomes more profitable.

Dynamic Strategy: Remember, the ideal capital structure is not static. It evolves with your business. Continually reassessing and adjusting your capital structure can help maximize shareholder wealth.

Your capital structure decisions have a direct impact on your shareholders' wealth. By understanding and managing this balance, you can build a financially stable and prosperous business that benefits everyone involved.

B. Comparative Analysis of Different Capital Structures and Their Outcomes

In business, the capital structure you choose can significantly impact your company's financial health and growth potential. Let's compare different capital structures and their typical outcomes:

High Equity, Low Debt: This structure is often seen in startups or small businesses where the owner prefers full control. While it minimizes debt-related risks, it can limit growth opportunities due to less available capital.

Case:

Imagine a young entrepreneur, Alex, who starts a tech company with his savings. Preferring full control, Alex opts for a high equity, low debt capital structure. He reinvests profits back into the business, avoiding loans. This approach keeps debt risks low, but as his company grows, Alex faces a challenge: he needs more funds for expansion but is hesitant to take on debt or sell shares to investors. While he maintains control, the company's growth pace is slow compared to competitors who leverage debt for rapid expansion. Alex's case illustrates how a high equity, low debt approach can secure control and minimize risks but may limit growth due to constrained capital.

Balanced Equity and Debt: Many successful businesses aim for this balance. It allows for growth through borrowed capital while maintaining a safety net through equity. This structure can optimize shareholder returns if managed well.

Case:

Imagine a thriving restaurant business, "Delish Diners," started by a passionate chef, Emily. Initially, Emily funded the business using her savings, avoiding debt to maintain full control. As Delish Diners gained popularity, Emily saw an opportunity to expand but needed more capital.

She decided on a balanced capital structure: part of the expansion was financed through a small business loan (debt), while the rest was funded by reinvesting profits (equity). This balance allowed Delish Diners to open new locations without overburdening the business with debt.

The loan brought in additional funds for renovations and marketing, contributing to increased customer traffic. The equity portion ensured that Emily retained significant control over business decisions and culture, which was crucial for her.

As Delish Diners grew, the profits increased, pleasing the shareholders, including Emily. The debt was manageable, not overwhelming the business's finances, and the increased profits from the expansion helped pay it off gradually.

This story of Delish Diners illustrates the power of a balanced capital structure. It provided the necessary capital for growth while maintaining the stability and control crucial for the business's success. This balance ultimately led to increased shareholder value, demonstrating the effectiveness of a well-managed combination of debt and equity in business expansion.

High Debt, Low Equity: Used by companies aiming for rapid expansion. While it can lead to significant growth, it also comes with high risk. If the business faces downturns, high debt repayments can strain finances, potentially reducing shareholder value.

Case:

Imagine a company, "TechGrow," aiming to become a major player in the tech industry rapidly. To achieve this, TechGrow opts for a high debt, low equity capital structure. They take out substantial loans to invest in cutting-edge technology, hire top talent, and expand their market reach. Initially, this approach seems successful, as TechGrow grows faster than its competitors.

However, the tech market suddenly faces a downturn. Tech-Grow's revenues decline, but its debt repayments remain high. The company struggles to manage these repayments, leading to financial strain. Shareholders, who initially saw their share value increase due to rapid growth, now face the risk of significant losses. TechGrow's story exemplifies the risks associated with a high debt, low equity structure, especially when external market conditions change unfavorably.

Each structure has its pros and cons. The key is to choose one that aligns with your business goals, risk tolerance, and industry norms. Remember, what works for one company may not work for another. Adaptability and continuous reassessment are crucial in capital structure management.

C. Strategies for optimizing capital structure for wealth maximization

Creating an optimal capital structure is essential for maximizing wealth in your business. Here's a detailed strategy for you as an entrepreneur:

Understanding Risk and Reward: The balance between debt and equity in your business is crucial. More debt can mean higher returns when things go well but can also increase the risk. Equity might be safer but can dilute your control. Consider your comfort with risk and the potential for rewards.

Industry Benchmarking: Different industries have varying norms for capital structure. Research your industry to understand what's typical and use it as a starting point. For example, tech startups often rely more on equity, while manufacturing firms might use more debt.

Stage of Business: Startups might not have steady cash flows to handle debt, so equity is often preferable. As your business matures and cash flows become more predictable, incorporating more debt might be feasible and beneficial.

Advantage of Debt: Debt can be an effective tool for growth, especially when interest rates are low. The interest on debt is often tax-deductible, which can lower your overall tax liability. However, it's important not to over-leverage to avoid financial strain.

Equity Financing: Issuing new equity can be a way to raise funds without incurring debt. However, it dilutes ownership. Use it wisely, especially when you need significant capital for growth that debt financing cannot fully provide.

Maintaining Flexibility: A flexible capital structure allows you to adapt to changes in the business environment. It's important to have the ability to switch between debt and equity financing as circumstances change.

Regular Review: The business environment is dynamic, and so should be your capital structure. Regularly review your debt-to-equity ratio. Be ready to adjust your strategy in response to changes in market conditions, interest rates, and your business growth.

Managing Debt Levels: Keep a close eye on your debt levels.

High debt can lead to financial distress, especially if your business hits hard times. Develop a plan for debt reduction if your debt-to-equity ratio becomes too high.

Investor Relations: Communicate your capital structure strategy to your investors. They need to understand how you are managing risks and pursuing growth. Transparency can build investor confidence.

Leverage Growth Opportunities: Use your capital structure to leverage growth opportunities. This might mean taking on debt to finance an expansion or using equity to fund a risky but potentially high-reward project.

Optimizing your capital structure is about finding the right balance that suits your business's unique needs and goals. It's a careful blend of risk management and growth pursuit. As you navigate through your entrepreneurial journey, keep reassessing and fine-tuning your capital structure to ensure it aligns with your evolving business strategy and market conditions. This approach will help you maximize shareholder wealth and ensure long-term success.

4

The Fund Utilization Principle

Definition and Importance of the Fund Utilization Principle

Recall the curiosity we sparked earlier about the Fund Utilization Principle? It's time to dive in. This principle is a vital guideline for entrepreneurs like you, concerning how to generate and use funds effectively.

The Principle Explained: At its core, the Fund Utilization Principle suggests using short-term funds for immediate or short-term needs, like managing day-to-day operations. Long-term funds, on the other hand, should be allocated for long-term investments, such as expanding your business, purchasing significant assets, or research and development.

Do's and Don'ts: It's crucial to adhere to this principle to maintain financial health. Using short-term funds for long-term purposes can lead to liquidity issues, as these funds will need to be repaid quickly.

Special Consideration: There is an exception – long-term funds can be used for short-term purposes if they are specifically raised for this reason, a strategy known as "Shoring up of Net Working Capital." This means if you've secured long-term funds with the intention of supporting short-term requirements, it's acceptable to use them as such. However, this should be the exception, not the norm.

The importance of the Fund Utilization Principle cannot be overstated. It's about smartly managing your resources to avoid financial pitfalls and ensuring that every dollar is optimally used for the growth and stability of your business. Remember, mismanagement of funds is a common reason for business difficulties. As an entrepreneur, applying this principle effectively can be your safeguard against such financial missteps.

B. Different forms of funds (short-term and long-term) and their characteristics

In understanding the Fund Utilization Principle, it's crucial for you, as an entrepreneur, to recognize the different forms of funds – short-term and long-term – and their characteristics.

Short-Term Funds:

Definition and Sources: Short-term funds are typically borrowed or accessed for a period of less than a year. Sources include bank overdrafts, trade credit, short-term loans, and money from marketable securities.

Usage: Ideal for managing daily operations like inventory purchases, payroll, and other operational expenses.

Characteristics: They usually have higher interest rates compared to long-term funds but provide greater flexibility. They are best used when quick repayment is possible from immediate revenues.

Long-Term Funds:

Definition and Sources: Long-term funds are accessed for a period longer than a year. Sources include long-term loans, bonds, retained earnings, and equity capital.

Usage: Suited for long-term investments like business expansion, large projects, purchasing significant assets, or research and development.

Characteristics: These funds typically have lower interest rates compared to short-term funds and are crucial for sustained growth. They provide stability and are essential for strategic, long-term business objectives.

Comparing the Two:

Risk Factor: Short-term funds carry a higher risk due to their immediate repayment requirements. In contrast, long-term funds, while lower in risk, require careful planning as they affect your business's financial leverage over a longer period.

Impact on Cash Flow: Mismanagement of short-term funds can quickly lead to cash flow problems. Long-term funds, if used wisely, can improve cash flow stability over time.

Cost Implications: The cost of short-term funds can be higher in the short run but doesn't accumulate much over time. Long-term funds, due to their extended nature, can accumulate significant interest costs over their lifespan.

Strategic Considerations for Entrepreneurs:

Balancing the Mix: Your focus should be on maintaining a healthy mix of short and long-term funds based on your business cycle, operational needs, and growth plans.

Understanding Your Business Cycle: Align your funding types with your business cycle. Use short-term funds for seasonal or cyclical needs and long-term funds for steady, year-round activities.

Flexibility and Preparedness: Maintain flexibility in your capital structure to adapt to changing market conditions. Be prepared with a plan to shift your funding sources as needed.

Understanding and effectively managing these two types of funds is vital for the financial health and growth of your business. Each type has its role, benefits, and risks. As an entrepreneur, your ability to skillfully balance short-term and long-term funds can significantly contribute to your business's success and longevity.

C. Guidelines for raising funds in alignment with business goals

Raising funds in alignment with your business goals is a critical step in your entrepreneurial journey. To do this effectively, you need to

1. Understand Your Business Goals
2. Assess Your Current Financial Position
3. Choose the Right Type of Funding
4. Explore Various Funding Sources
5. Consider the Cost of Capital
6. Maintain a Good Credit Score
7. Understand Legal and Tax Implications
8. Plan for Repayment
9. Monitor and Adjust as Needed

Let's understand in detail.

1) Understand Your Business Goals: Understanding your business goals is like setting the destination for a journey. As an entrepreneur, you need to define where you want your business to go. This means setting clear short-term and long-term objectives.

Short-term goals might include boosting sales for the next quarter, launching a new product, or improving your customer service. These are immediate targets that often require quick funding solutions to seize opportunities or address challenges.

Long-term objectives could involve expanding your business into new markets, investing in major technological upgrades, or scaling up your operations. These goals are your vision for the business's future and usually require a larger, more sustained investment.

Your funding needs directly correlate with these goals. For short-term objectives, you might look for flexible, quick funding options. For long-term goals, you'll likely need more substantial funding sources that align with the scope and scale of your ambitions. In both cases, the right funding not only supports your goals but also sets a stable financial foundation for your business's growth.

2) Assess Your Current Financial Position: When assessing your financial position, a detailed analysis of your assets, liabilities, and cash flow is vital, along with relevant financial ratios.

Let's consider 'TechStart', a small tech company:

- *Assets and Liabilities:* TechStart's current assets are $100,000, and its liabilities are $50,000.
- *Cash Flow:* Monthly cash inflow is $20,000 and outflow is $15,000, leading to a positive cash flow of $5,000.

Key Financial Ratios:

- *Current Ratio (Assets / Liabilities):* TechStart's ratio is 2 ($100,000 / $50,000), indicating good liquidity.
- *Debt-to-Equity Ratio (Liabilities / Equity):* If equity is $70,000, the ratio is 0.71 ($50,000 / $70,000), showing a healthy balance between debt and equity.
- *Cash Flow Margin (Cash Flow from Operations / Net Sales):* At 25% ($5,000 / $20,000), it reflects efficient cash manage-

ment.

Combining these insights, TechStart has robust short-term financial health, a balanced level of debt and equity, and efficient operations. However, it should be cautious about adding long-term debt, which could disrupt this balance. This analysis assists in making informed decisions about the type and amount of funding suitable for the company's needs.

Let's imagine another business, 'StruggleTech,' and how its financial health looks quite different.

- Picture StruggleTech with only $40,000 in the bank but owing $50,000 soon. That's like having less in your wallet than your monthly bills – a current ratio of 0.8.
- Now, think of them having big loans, say $250,000, while their total investment in the business is only $50,000. This means they're heavily relying on borrowed money – their debt-to-equity ratio is alarmingly high at 5.
- Also, they're making $40,000 in sales but only keeping $2,000 of it, a slim 5% margin.

For a business owner, these numbers are red flags. StruggleTech needs to rethink its spending, maybe try to ease its loan terms, or find new investment to get back on solid ground.

3) Choose the Right Type of Funding:

Choosing the right type of funding is a bit like picking the right tool for a job. As an entrepreneur, you need to decide between short-term and long-term funding based on your business's specific needs.

Short-Term Funding: This is like a quick fix. It's perfect when you need cash fast for immediate needs like covering a temporary cash flow gap, financing a short-term project, or dealing with unexpected expenses. These funds are typically easier to obtain but need to be paid back quickly.

Long-Term Funding: Think of this as an investment in your business's future. It's ideal for significant, long-term plans like expanding your business, buying major equipment, or investing in R&D. Long-term funding usually involves larger amounts and takes longer to repay, but it's essential for growth that takes time to show results.

Your choice depends on the nature of your need – is it immediate or strategic? Always align your funding choice with your business goals and the time frame you're working within.

Sample Q&A for better understanding of Funding Types for Business Scenarios

Q: What type of funding should I use for launching a marketing campaign?

A: Short-term funding is ideal for covering immediate marketing expenses.

Q: Is it better to use short-term or long-term funding for purchasing inventory for peak season?

A: Use short-term funding to buy inventory needed for a seasonal sales increase.

Q: What type of funding should I use for expanding to a new location?

A: Opt for long-term funding for significant investments in new premises and equipment.

Q: Should I choose long-term funding for upgrading technology systems?

A: Yes, choose long-term funding as this is a substantial investment that benefits the business over many years.

Q: What's the best funding option for covering payroll during a slow season?

A: Short-term funding is suitable for managing temporary cash flow shortages.

Q: What kind of funding is appropriate for research and development of new products?

A: Long-term funding is needed due to the extended nature of R&D projects.

Q: Should I use long-term funding for renovating business premises?

A: Yes, as renovations are a significant investment with long-term benefits, long-term funding is appropriate.

Q: What type of funding should be used for paying off a short-term debt?

A: Short-term funding is best for quickly clearing existing short-term obligations.

Q: For buying a major piece of equipment, which funding should I consider?

A: Long-term funding is suitable as it's a substantial investment providing long-term value.

General Guideline:

- Use short-term funds for operational expenses or short-term goals, ensuring these can be repaid quickly from your business's cash flow.
- Opt for long-term funding for significant investments or projects that will drive growth and revenue over an extended period, where the benefits and returns are realized over several years.

4) Explore Various Funding Sources

Exploring various funding sources is key to finding the right financial support for your business. Each source has its own advantages and fits different needs.

Banks: Traditional but reliable. Banks offer loans with various terms and rates. Good for both short-term and long-term needs, but they usually require strong credit history and collateral.

Investors: These can be angel investors or venture capitalists. They provide funding in exchange for equity in your business. Great for long-term growth, especially if you're willing to share control and profits.

Crowdfunding: A modern approach where you raise small amounts of money from many people, typically via the internet. Good for projects that resonate with the public.

Government Grants and Loans: Sometimes overlooked,

these can be a great source, especially for startups or specific industries. They often have favorable terms.

Peer-to-Peer Lending: This is borrowing from individuals without going through a traditional financial institution. It's flexible but can come with higher interest rates.

Each option has its nuances, so consider what aligns best with your business model and growth plans.

5) Consider the Cost of Capital

Understanding the cost of capital is like comparing different paths to climb a mountain. Each path has its own challenges and benefits.

Imagine you're considering a loan for your business. The cost here is the interest rate. If it's low, it's like a smooth path with a gentle slope. But remember, even a low rate adds up over time, like a longer trek.

Now, think about getting an investor. They might not charge interest, but they'll want equity – a share in your business. It's like having a partner on your climb. They help you up, but you'll share the view at the top.

So, choosing the right option is about balancing cost and flexibility. A loan might be cheaper short-term, but equity could bring valuable long-term support. It's about picking the path that fits your journey best.

Let's consider two examples to further understand the cost of capital:

Loan for Equipment Purchase: Suppose you need to buy new machinery. You find a loan with a 5% interest rate. It seems manageable, but calculate the total cost over the loan period. If it's a $50,000 loan over five years, you're looking at significant interest payments. But, the equipment could boost efficiency, balancing the cost.

Equity Funding for Expansion: You're planning to expand your business. An investor offers $100,000 for a 10% stake. No interest, but you're giving up a share of future profits and some control. If your business doubles in value, that 10% becomes much more valuable. It's a trade-off: no interest for shared success and additional expertise.

In each scenario, weigh the immediate and long-term costs against the potential benefits. It's about finding the best fit for your business's current needs and future growth.

6) Maintain a Good Credit Score

Keeping a good credit score is like maintaining a strong reputation. It's crucial, especially when you want to take out loans for your business. Think of your credit score as your financial report card. Just like you'd manage your business's debts smartly, do the same with your personal or business loans. Pay bills on time, don't overextend your credit, and keep a check on your credit reports. A strong credit score can open doors to better loan terms and rates, making it easier and more cost-effective to grow your business.

7) Understand Legal and Tax Implications

When you're choosing how to fund your business, it's vital to consider the legal and tax implications. Each funding method can affect your business differently in terms of taxes.

For example, if you take a loan, the interest you pay might be tax-deductible, reducing your taxable income. But, if you go for equity funding, it doesn't offer such immediate tax benefits. Legally, equity investors may have a say in your business decisions, unlike lenders. Also, different funding methods may have various regulatory requirements.

So, it's important to understand these aspects to avoid surprises later. Good legal and tax advice is essential here to navigate these complexities effectively.

8) Plan for repayment

When you borrow funds for your business, having a solid repayment plan is like setting a reliable roadmap for a journey. First, thoroughly understand your business's cash flow cycles. Know when and how much cash comes in and goes out. This helps you plan your repayments around times when you have more cash at hand, making sure you're not caught off-guard.

In the second step, consider the unpredictability of business. Sometimes, sales might dip or unexpected expenses may crop up. Here, contingency planning comes into play. It's like having a spare tire in your trunk. Maybe you set aside a portion of profits into an emergency fund or arrange for a line of credit as a backup. This ensures that even in tough times, you can keep up with repayments.

Finally, always keep communication lines open with your lenders. If you foresee challenges in repayment, it's better to discuss restructuring options proactively rather than missing payments. Being upfront can build trust and might lead to more flexible terms. Your aim should be to maintain a strong credit score and good relations with lenders, as they are crucial assets for your business's financial health.

9) Monitor and Adjust as Needed

Monitoring and adjusting your financial strategy is like navigating a ship through changing seas. It's essential to keep a close eye on your business's financial performance regularly. This means regularly reviewing your profit margins, cash flow statements, and how effectively the funding is contributing to your business goals. Are you seeing the growth or stability you expected? If not, it may be time to adjust your sails.

As the market and your business evolve, so should your financial strategies. This could mean shifting from short-term to long-term funding, reconsidering your investment plans, or even changing your business model.

Continuously monitoring and adjusting your financial strategy is vital for your business's success. It's like being a captain who constantly checks the compass and adjusts the course. Regularly review your financial statements to gauge your business's performance. Are you meeting your profit targets? Is your cash flow steady? How effectively is the funding helping you achieve your goals? If things aren't going as planned, don't hesitate to change your approach.

The business world is ever-changing, so your strategies should be flexible. This might mean adjusting your funding sources, changing investment priorities, or even pivoting your business model.

D. Strategies for managing and monitoring funds effectively

Managing and monitoring your funds effectively is key in applying the Fund Utilization Principle to your business:

Set Clear Financial Objectives: Begin by defining specific and measurable financial goals. This will provide a clear target for how you should manage and allocate your funds.

Develop a Budget: Create a detailed budget that aligns with your financial objectives. This will help you track your income and expenses, ensuring you stay on course.

Regular Financial Review: Schedule regular reviews of your financial statements. This enables you to monitor your business's financial health and make adjustments as needed.

Utilize Financial Management Tools: Implement accounting software or financial management tools. These can automate various aspects of financial tracking, making it easier to monitor cash flow and expenses.

Maintain Liquidity and Emergency Funds: Ensure you have enough liquidity for daily operations and an emergency fund for unforeseen expenses. This helps in maintaining financial stability in your business.

By following these strategies, you can effectively manage and monitor your funds, paving the way for sound financial health and growth in your business.

E. Avoiding misallocation and optimizing fund utilization

Optimizing fund utilization and avoiding misallocation are critical for the financial health of your business. As an entrepreneur, ensuring that every dollar in your business is used effectively is key. Misallocation of funds can lead to cash flow problems and inhibit growth. Let's break down how you can optimize fund utilization and avoid common pitfalls.

Avoid Using Short-Term Funds for Long-Term Purposes: One cardinal rule in fund management is not to use short-term funds for long-term purposes. Short-term funds are like your daily operational cash – using them for big, long-term projects can leave you struggling to cover everyday expenses.

Effective Budgeting: Create a budget that aligns with your business goals and stick to it. This will help you allocate funds effectively, ensuring that resources are used for their intended purposes.

Monitoring Cash Flow: Keep a close eye on your cash flow. Regular monitoring will help you identify any discrepancies between your planned and actual expenditures, allowing for timely adjustments.

Investing in Growth Opportunities: When allocating funds for growth, be strategic. Invest in areas that offer the best return on investment and align with your long-term business strategy.

Contingency Planning: Always have a contingency plan for unexpected expenses or shifts in the market. This ensures that unforeseen events don't derail your financial plans.

Proper fund utilization and avoiding misallocation are essential for the success of your business. By following these strategies, you can ensure that your business remains financially healthy, agile, and positioned for growth. Remember, the way you manage your funds can make a significant difference in achieving your business objectives.

5

Smart Funding Strategies

Tailoring capital structure to business lifecycle and industry

Tailoring your capital structure to fit your business lifecycle and industry is crucial. Think of your business like a growing organism, changing needs at each stage of its life.

Startup Phase: In the early days, when risk is high and cash flow uncertain, equity financing might be safer. You could turn to personal savings, family, friends, or angel investors. This avoids heavy debt burdens when your business is still finding its footing.

Growth Phase: As your business grows and cash flow becomes more predictable, you can start incorporating debt. This can fuel expansion, such as entering new markets or increasing production capacity. Loans or lines of credit are common choices here.

Maturity Phase: In a mature business stage, maintaining a balanced mix of debt and equity is key. You might consider long-term debt for major investments like acquiring another company or launching a new product line.

Industry Considerations: Your industry also plays a role. High-growth industries like technology may favor equity to avoid stifling growth with debt repayments. More stable sectors, like manufacturing, might lean more on debt financing.

Remember, there's no one-size-fits-all approach. Continuously assess your business's position and adjust your capital structure accordingly, keeping an eye on industry trends and growth prospects.

B. Mitigating risks associated with different funding sources

When using different funding sources, it's crucial to mitigate risks to ensure the financial health of your business.

Equity Financing: This involves selling a share of your business. It's vital to understand that while it doesn't require regular repayments like a loan, it does dilute your ownership. Be cautious about how much equity you give away – retaining control of your business is key.

Debt Financing: Loans need to be repaid with interest. Manage these risks by not over-borrowing and ensuring your cash flow can comfortably cover repayments. Also, keep an eye on interest rates and try to lock in lower rates when possible.

Venture Capital: While this can bring in substantial funds, it often comes with expectations of high growth and returns. Ensure you're aligned with your investors on business goals and growth trajectories.

Crowdfunding: This method can be beneficial but manage expectations carefully. Be transparent with your backers about timelines and potential risks involved in your project.

Government Grants and Subsidies: While often seen as 'free money,' they come with specific conditions and usage restrictions. Ensure compliance with these terms to avoid legal or financial repercussions.

Each funding source has its unique risks. Balancing them with the potential benefits and aligning them with your business strategy and capabilities is crucial.

6

Common Financial MistakestoAvoid

Identifying pitfalls in capital structure decisions

Making wise capital structure decisions is crucial for your business's financial health. Here are some common pitfalls to avoid:

Overreliance on Debt: While debt can fuel growth, too much of it can strain your cash flow and increase financial risk. Ensure your debt levels are manageable and aligned with your company's ability to generate revenue.

Ignoring Industry Norms: Every industry has its own financial benchmarks. Ignoring these can lead you to adopt a capital structure that's unsuitable for your sector. Understand and consider industry standards when making decisions.

Neglecting Financial Ratios: Key financial ratios, like debt-to-equity and interest coverage ratios, offer insights into your financial health. Overlooking these can lead to imbalances in your capital structure that might go unnoticed until they become problematic.

Lack of Flexibility: The market and your business needs will evolve. A rigid capital structure can limit your ability to adapt to changes. Ensure your approach allows for adjustments in response to new opportunities or challenges.

Underestimating the Importance of Equity: Relying too much on debt and not considering equity options can lead to problems. Equity

Relying too much on debt and not considering equity options can lead to problems. Equity doesn't just dilute ownership; it can bring in strategic partners and open growth opportunities. Balancing equity and debt according to your business's phase and market conditions is key.

B. Real-world examples of financial mistakes and their consequences

Learning from real-world financial missteps can be incredibly instructive. Let's look at some examples from the USA, UK, and India, where poor capital structure decisions led to significant consequences:

Carillion (UK): This British construction giant collapsed due to massive debts and an overstretched business model. The company took on risky projects, financed largely through debt, which didn't yield the expected returns. This led to its inability to service its debts, eventually causing its downfall.

Kingfisher Airlines (India): This airline's failure is attributed to its aggressive expansion funded by high levels of debt. The company failed to generate enough revenue to cover its costs and debt payments. This misalignment between its ambitious growth plans and financial reality led to its collapse.

Jet Airways (India): The airline struggled due to high levels of debt and intense competition, leading to its eventual grounding and bankruptcy proceedings.

Debenhams (UK): This well-known British retailer went into administration following high debts and failure to keep up with the evolving retail landscape.

Blockbuster (USA): The video rental giant failed to adapt to the digital era and struggled under significant debt, leading to its eventual bankruptcy.

Nortel Networks (Canada): This telecommunications and data networking equipment manufacturer faced bankruptcy due to an unsustainable debt load and financial mismanagement.

C. Lessons learned from entrepreneurial failures

Learning from entrepreneurial failures is like gathering wisdom from others' experiences. Here are key lessons:

Understand Your Market: It's vital to deeply understand your market and adapt accordingly. Many businesses fail due to a lack of market knowledge or ignoring market changes.

Manage Finances Prudently: Mismanagement of funds is a common pitfall. Keep a close eye on your expenses and revenue streams. Overleveraging or poor cash flow management can lead to financial distress.

Avoid Overexpansion: Expanding too quickly without a solid foundation or plan can lead to failure. Grow your business sustainably, ensuring each step is financially viable.

Embrace Flexibility: The business world is dynamic. Be ready to pivot your strategy if your current approach isn't working. Flexibility can be the difference between surviving and failing.

Learn from Mistakes: Every failure has a lesson. Whether it's your own business or another's, there's always something to learn. Use these lessons to refine your strategies and avoid similar pitfalls in the future.

7

Conclusion

Let's recap the key concepts and strategies:

Smart Funding Strategies: Tailoring your capital structure to your business's lifecycle and industry is crucial. Balancing different funding sources while mitigating associated risks ensures financial stability and growth.

Capital Structure: Understanding and managing the mix of debt and equity in your business is vital. The right balance can lead to wealth maximization and sustainable growth.

Fund Utilization: Using short-term funds for short-term needs and long-term funds for long-term goals is a fundamental principle. Adhering to this helps in maintaining financial health.

Avoiding Financial Mistakes: Learning from common financial errors, like over-leveraging or ignoring market changes, is essential. Real-world examples offer valuable lessons in what to avoid.

Adaptability and Learning: Stay flexible and adaptable. Continuously learn from both successes and failures, and adjust your strategies accordingly for ongoing success.

These insights can guide you in making informed financial decisions, ultimately steering your business towards prosperity.

B. Encouraging entrepreneurs to apply learned principles to their businesses

As we wrap up, here's some encouragement for you, the entrepreneur, to apply these principles to your business:

Integrate the Strategies: Implement smart funding strategies by understanding your unique business cycle and industry norms. Each business is different, and your approach should reflect your specific situation.

Balance Your Capital Structure: Pay close attention to your mix of debt and equity. This balance is crucial for maintaining financial health and driving growth.

Apply Fund Utilization Principles: Use short-term funds for immediate needs and long-term funds for strategic growth. Proper fund utilization is key to avoiding cash flow issues.

Learn from Others: Take lessons from both successful ventures and failures. Understand what worked for others and what didn't, and apply these insights to your business.

Stay Flexible and Adaptable: The business world is ever-changing. Be ready to adjust your strategies and learn continuously. This adaptability is crucial for long-term success.

Remember, the principles and strategies discussed are not just theories but practical tools to guide you on your entrepreneurial journey. Implementing them effectively can set your business on a path to growth and stability.

C. Closing thoughts on the journey towards wealth maximization through smart funding.

Let's reflect on the journey towards wealth maximization through smart funding:

Empowerment through Knowledge: The journey begins with understanding. Equip yourself with the knowledge of how different funding strategies affect your business's growth and stability.

Strategic Planning: Use this knowledge to strategically plan your capital structure. Balance short-term and long-term funding to support your business goals effectively.

Prudent Financial Management: Exercise caution in financial management. Avoid common pitfalls and learn from both your experiences and those of others.

Adaptability is Key: The business landscape is dynamic. Stay adaptable, continuously reassess your strategies, and be ready to pivot when necessary.

Path to Success: Remember, smart funding isn't just about securing resources; it's about wisely managing them to maximize wealth and ensure the long-term success of your entrepreneurial venture.

Keep these closing thoughts in mind as you navigate your path to success. The journey of entrepreneurship is challenging, but with the right financial strategies, you can achieve sustainable growth and wealth maximization.

About the Author

CA N Raja, a Chartered Accountant by qualification and corporate trainer by passion, initially served as an Assistant Vice President in Credit at the State Bank of India, where he garnered expertise in financial analysis, risk assessment, and project finance over four years.

Following his banking career, he launched his CA practice and began instructing CA and CMA students in financial management and strategic financial management. Seven and a half years later, he embarked on edupreneurship, establishing CA Raja Classes, an eLearning platform that imparts knowledge in financial analysis, credit analysis, and financial management to professionals, students, and finance executives.

To date, CA N Raja has educated more than 250,000 students through over 100 online courses, written numerous ebooks on financial analysis, and amassed a substantial YouTube following of 138,000 plus subscribers for his educational video lectures.

You can connect with me on:

- https://carajaclasses.com
- https://www.linkedin.com/in/carajaclasses
- https://www.youtube.com/carajaclasses